My First
AMHARIC
DICTIONARY

ENGLISH-AMHARIC

D1609689

Designed and edited by Maria Watson
Translated by Tsegazeab Hailegebriel

Hippocrene Books, Inc.
New York

My First Amharic Dictionary

English-Amharic

Hippocrene Books, Inc. edition, 2019

For information, address:
HIPPOCRENE BOOKS, INC.
171 Madison Avenue
New York, NY 10016
www.hippocrenebooks.com

ISBN: 978-0-7818-1402-7

First edition, 2019

Published by arrangement with Biblio Bee Publications, an imprint of ibs Books (UK)
56, Langland Crescent, Stanmore HA7 1NG, U.K.

Printed at Star Print-O-Bind, New Delhi-110 020 (India)

Aa

actor

ተዋናይ   tewanayi

actress

ተዋናይት   tewanayit

adult

አዋቂ   awaqi

aeroplane
US English **airplane**

አውሮፕላን
ewroplan

air conditioner

አየር ማጣዣ
eyer mateeźa

air hostess
US English **flight attendant**

ሴት የበረራ አስተናጋጅ
yeberera 'estenagaĵ

airport

አውሮፕላን ማረፊያ
awiropyelan marafiya

album

የፎቶግራፍ ማኖሪያ
yefotogiraf manoriya

almond

ለውዝ   laweze

alphabet

ፊደል   fideli

ambulance

አምቡላንስ   ambulanisi

a b c d e f g h i j k l m n o p q r s t u v w x y z

a b c d e f g h i J k l m n o p q r s t u v w x y z

angel
መልአክ   melak

animal
እንስሳ   ensisa

ankle
ቁርጭምጭሚት
kurichimichimīti

ant
ጉንዳን   gundaan

antelope
አጋዘን   agazeni

antenna
አንቴና   antina

apartment
አፓርታማ   apartama

ape
ጦጣ   tota

apple
ፖም   pomi

apricot

አፕሪኮች   aprikochi

apron

ሸርጥ   shiriṭ

aquarium

ያሳ ማስቀመጫ ገንዳy
a'sa masqemeča genda

archery

ቀስት   kesite

architect

ፕላን ነዳፊ   pilan nedafi

arm

ክንድ   kinid

armour
US English **armor**

ጋሻ   gasha

arrow

ቀስት   kesite

artist

ሰአሊ   seali

asparagus

አስፓራጉስ   'esparagus

astronaut

ጠፈርተኛ   tefertegna

astronomer

የሥነ ፈለክ ተመራማሪ
ye'sne felek temeramari

athlete

ስፖርተኛ   siportegna

atlas

አትላስ   atilasi

aunt

አክስት   'ekst

author

ደራሲ   derasi

automobile

መኪና   mekina

autumn

በልግ   belg

avalanche

የበረዶ ናዳ
yeberedo nada

award

ሽልማት   shilimate

axe

መጥረቢያ   metirebiyaa

baby

ሕፃን   ẍxan

back

ጀርባ   jeriba

bacon

በእንፉሎት የደረቀ ያሣማ ሥጋ
be'ènfulot yedereqe
ya'sama 'sga

badge

የመለያ ምልክት
yemeleya mlkt

badminton

ባድሚንተን
badminten

bag

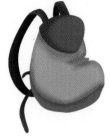

ቦርሳ   borsa

baker

ዳቦ ጋጋሪ   dabo gagari

balcony

ሰገነት   segenet

bald

መላጣ   melata

ball

ኳስ   kuas

ballerina

ባለሪና ዳንሰኛ
balerina dancegna

balloon

ፊኛ   figna

bamboo

ሽንበቆ   shenibek'o

banana

ሙዝ   muz

band

ባንድ   bandi

bandage

የቁሰል መጠቅለያ
yequsel meteqleya

barbeque

የፍም ጥብስ
yefim tibs

a
b
c
d
e
f
g
h
i
j
k
l
m
n
o
p
q
r
s
t
u
v
w
x
y
z

barn

ጋጣ   gata

barrel

በርሜል   bermel

baseball

ቤዝቦል   bezbol

basket

ቅርጫት   qirchat

basketball

ቅርጫት ኳስ
qirchat kuas

bat

የሌሊት ወፍ
yelelit wef

bath

መታጠቢያ   metatebiya

battery

ባትሪ   batiri

bay

ባህረ ሰላጤ
behre selatee

beach

ባሕር ዳር   baḥiri dari

beak

መንቆር   menkor

bean

ባቄላ   baqela

bear

ድብ   dib

beard

ጢም   tim

bed

አልጋ   aliga

bee

ንብ   nib

beetle

ጥንዚዛ   tiniziza

beetroot

ቀይስር   qey sir

bell

ደወል   deweli

belt

ቀበቶ   qebeto

berry

እንጆሪ   einjori

bicycle

ብስክሌት   biskilet

billiards
US English **pool**

ቢላዋርድ   bīlawaridi

bin

መጣያ   met'aya

a b c d e f g h i J k l m n o p q r s t u v w x y z

9

a
b
c
d
e
f
g
h
i
j
k
l
m
n
o
p
q
r
s
t
u
v
w
x
y
z

bird

ወፍ   wef

biscuit

ብስኩት   biskut

black

ጥቁር   tikur

blackboard

ጥቁር ሰሌዳ
ẗqur seleeda

blanket

ብርድ ልብስ
bird libs

blizzard

ኃይለኛ ነፋስ
hayleǹa nefus

blood

ደም   dem

blue

ሰማያዊ   semayawii

boat

ጀልባ   jelba

body

ሰውነት   sewinet

bone

አጥንት   atint

book

መጽሀፍ   mexħef

boot

ቦት ጫማ   bot čama

bottle

ጠርሙስ   termus

bow

የቢራቢሮ ቅርጽ
yebirabiro kirs

bowl

ድርብ ሳሕን   drb saẖn

box

ሳጥን   satin

boy

ወንድ ልጅ   wenidi liji

bracelet

አምባር   ambar

brain
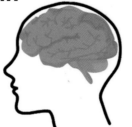
አንጎል   angol

branch

ቅርንጫፍ   qirinchaf

bread

ዳቦ   dabo

breakfast

ቁርስ   kurs

brick

ጡብ   ťubi

a
b
c
d
e
f
g
h
i
j
k
l
m
n
o
p
q
r
s
t
u
v
w
x
y
z

bride

ሙሽሪት   mushrit

bridegroom

ሙሽራ   mushra

bridge

ድልድይ   dildiy

broom

መጥረጊያ   metiregiya

brother

ወንድም   wendim

brown

ቡኒ   buni

brush

ብሩሽ   burush

bubble

አረፋ   arefaa

bucket

ባልዲ   baldi

buffalo

ጎሽ   goosh

building

ህንጻ   hintsa

bulb

አምፖል   ampol

bull

በሬ   beree

bun
ክብ ኬክ   kib kek

bunch

የአበቦች ስብስብ
ye'ābebochi sibisibi

bundle

ጥቅል   tiqil

bungalow
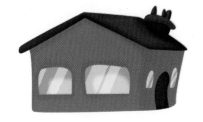
አነስተኛ ቤት
anestegna bet

burger

በርገር   berger

bus

አውቶቡስ   'ewtobus

bush

ቁጥቁጦ   qutquato

butcher

ስጋ ሻጭ   siga shach

butter

ቅቤ   qibe

butterfly

ቢራቢሮ   birabiro

button
አዝራር   azirar

a b c d e f g h i j J k l m n o p q r s t u v w x y z

Cc

cabbage

ጎመን   gomen

cabinet

ካቢኔ   kabine

cable

የብረት ገመድ
yebiret gemed

cable car

የኬብል መኪና
yekēbili mekīna

cactus

ቁልቁል   kulqual

cafe

ካፌ   kafe

cage

የወፍ ቤት   yewef beet

cake

ኬክ   kek

calculator

ማስሊያ   masliya

calendar

የቀን መቁጠሪያ
yeqen mekuteria

calf

ጥጃ   tija

camel

ግመል　　　gimel

camera

ካሜራ　　　kamera

camp

ሰፈር　　　sefer

can

በቆርቆሮ የታሸገ
bekorkoro yetashege

canal

ቦይ　　　boy

candle

ሻማ　　　shama

canoe

ታንኩአ　　　tankua

canteen

ምግብ ቤት　migibi bēti

cap

ቆብ　　　qob

captain

ካፒቴን　　　kapiten

car

መኪና　　　mekina

caravan

ከረቨን　　　kereven

a
b
c
d
e
f
g
h
i
j
k
l
m
n
o
p
q
r
s
t
u
v
w
x
y
z

card

ካርታ karta

carnival

ክብረ በዓል kibre beal

carpenter

አናጢ anati

carpet

ምንጣፍ mintaf

carrot

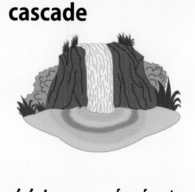

ካሮት karot

cart

ጋሪ garii

cartoon

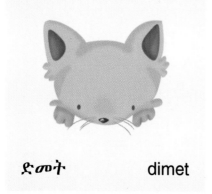

አሻንጎሊት eshangolit

cascade

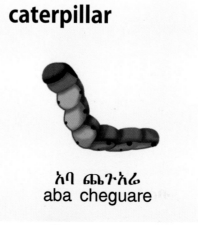

ፏፏቴ fwafwate

castle

ቤተ መንግስት
bēte menigisiti

cat

ድመት dimet

caterpillar

አባ ጨጉአሬ
aba cheguare

cauliflower

አበባ ጎመን
abeba gomen

cave
ዋሻ washa

ceiling
ጣሪያ tara

centipede
አምሳ እግር
'emsa 'ègr

centre
US English **center**
መሀል mehal

cereal
እህል ehil

chain
ሰንሰለት senselet

chair
ወንበር wenber

chalk
ጠመኔ temene

cheek
ጉንጭ gunch

cheese
አይብ ayiib

chef
አብሳይ 'ebsay

cherry
እንጀሪ einjori

chess

ቼዝ chēzi

chest

ደረት deret

chick

ጫጩት chachut

chilli
US English **chili**

ሚጥሚጣ mitmita

chimney

ጭስ ማውጫ
chis mawcha

chin

አገጭ agech

chocolate

ቸኮሌት chekolet

christmas

የገና በአል
yegena be'el

church

ቤተክርስቲያን
bete kirstian

cinema

ሲኒማ sinima

circle

ክብ kib

circus

ሰርከስ serkes

city

ከተማ   ketema

classroom

መማሪያ ክፍል
memariya kifl

clinic

ክሊኒክ   kilinik

clock

ሰዓት   seat

cloth

ጨርቅ   čerq

cloud

ደመና   demena

clown

አስቂኝ ተዋናይ
asqign tewanay

coal

ከሰል   kesel

coast

የባህር ዳርቻ
yebahir darcha

coat

ካፖርት   kaport

cobra

ኮብራ   kobra

cockerel
US English **rooster**

ጥንቸል   tinchel

a b **c** d e f g h i j k l m n o p q r s t u v w x y z

a b c d e f g h i J k l m n o p q r s t u v w x y z

cockroach

በረሮ   berero

coconut

ኮኮነት   kokonet

coffee

ቡና   buna

coin

ሳንቲም   santim

colour
US English **color**

ከለር   keler

comb

ማበጠሪያ   maberterya

comet

ጅራታም ኮከብ
jiratam kokeb

compass

ኮምፓስ   kompas

computer

ኮምፒውተር
kompiwter

cone

ሾጣጣ   shoïaïa

container

መክተቻ   mektecha

cook
አብሳይ   'ebsay

20

cookie

ኩኪ   kuki

cord

ገመድ   gemed

corn

በቆሎ   beqolo

cot

አልጋህን ተሽክመህ
'elgahn teshekmeh

cottage

ትንሽ መኖሪያ ቤት
nsh menoriya beet

cotton

ጥጥ   tiit

country

ሀገር   hager

couple

ጥንዶች   tindoch

court

ፍርድ ቤት   fird bet

cow

ላም   lam

crab

ሸርጣን   shertan

crane

ክሬን   kiren

crayon

በመቀባት
bemeqebat

crocodile

አዞ   azo

cross

መስቀል   meskel

crow

ቁራ   qura

crowd

ህዝብ   hizb

crown

ዘውድ   zewid

cube

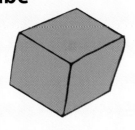

ኩብ   kub

cucumber

ክያር   kyar

cup

ኩባያ   kubaya

cupboard

ቁምሳጥን   kum satn

curtain

መጋረጃ   megareja

cushion

ትራስ   tiras

Dd

dam

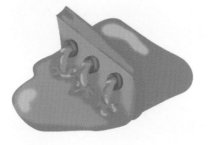

ግድብ   gidb

dancer

ዳንሰኛ   dansegna

dart

ዳርት   darit

data

መረጃ   mereja

dates

ቀጠሮ   qëtero

daughter

ሴት ልጅ   set lij

day

ቀን   qen

deck

የመርከብ ወለል
yemerkeb welel

deer

አጋዘን   agazen

den

መሸሸጊያ
mesheshegiya

dentist

የጥርስ ሀኪም
ye tirs hakim

a b c d e f g h i j k l m n o p q r s t u v w x y z

desert

በርሃ   berha

design

ንድፍ   nidifi

desk

የጽሕፈተ ጠረጴዛ
yexħfete ṫereṗeeza

dessert

ጣፋጭ ምግብ
ṫafuč mgb

detective

መርማሪ   mermari

diamond

አልማዝ   alimaz

diary

ማስታወሻ መያዣ ደብተር
mastawesha meyaźa debter

dice

ዛህራ   zahra

dictionary

መዝገበ ቃላት
mezgebe kalat

dinosaur

ዳይኖሰር   daynoser

disc

ዲስክ   disqi

dish

ሳህን   sahin

diver

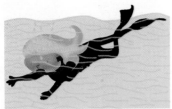

ጠላቂ   telaki

dock

የመርከብ ወደብ
yemerkeb wedeb

doctor

ሐኪም   ĥekim

dog

ውሻ   wusha

doll

አሻንጉሊት   ashangulit

dolphin

ዶልፊን   dolfin

dome

ጉልላት   gullat

domino

ዶሚኖ   dominoo

donkey

አህያ   ahiyaa

donut

ዶናት   donat

door

በር   ber

dough

ሊጥ   lit

dragon

ዘንዶ   zendo

drain

የውሃ ውራጅ
yewuha wiraj

drawer

መሳቢያ   mesabiya

drawing

ስዕል   seel

dream

ህልም   hilm

dress

ቀሚስ   qemis

drink

መጠጥ   meṭeṭ

driver

ሹፌር   shufer

drop

ጠብታ   tebita

drought

ድርቅ   dirk

drum

ከበሮ   kebero

duck

ዳክዬ   dakiye

dustbin
US English **trash can**

የቆሻሻ   yeqoshasha

duvet

ትንሽ አልጋ
tinsh alga

dwarf

ድንክ   dink

Ee

eagle

ንስር   nisir

ear

ጆሮ   joro

earring

የጆሮ ጌጥ
yejoro geet

earth

ምድር   midr

earthquake

የመሬት መንቀጥቀጥ
yemeret menketket

earthworm

የመሬት ትል
yemereet tl

eclipse

ግርዶሽ   grdosh

edge

ጠርዝ   terz

a b c d e f g h i J k l m n o p q r s t u v w x y z

eel

የዓሣ ዓይነት
ye'ä'sa 'äynet

egg

እንቁላል enkulal

eight

ስምንት simnt

elastic

ስለሚሳሳቡ
slemisasabu

elbow

ክርን kirn

electrician

የኢሌክትሪክ ባለሙያ
yeelektrik balemuya

electricity

ኢሌክትሪክ elektrik

elephant

ዝሆን zihon

elevator

አሳንሰር asanser

elf

ትንሽ ተንኮለኛ
tinsh tenkolegna

email

እጦማር eṫomar

embroidery

ጥልፍ tilf

engine
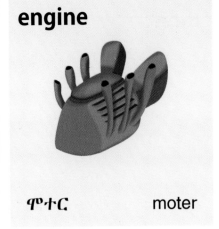
ሞተር   moter

entrance
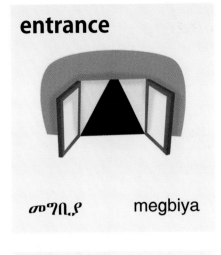
መግቢያ   megbiya

envelope

ፖስታ   posta

equator
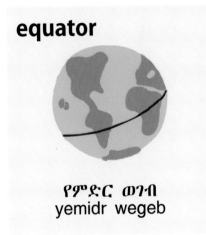
የምድር ወገብ
yemidr wegeb

equipment

መሳሪያ   mesariya

eraser
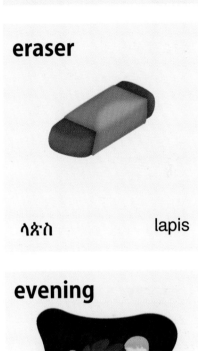
ላጲስ   lapis

escalator

የሚንቀሳቀስ ደረጃ
yeminqesaqes dereĵa

eskimo

ኤስኪሞ   iskimo

evening

ምሽት   mishit

exhibition

ኢግዚቢሽን   igzibishn

eye
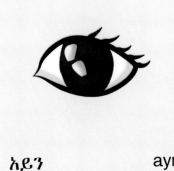
አይን   ayn

eyebrow
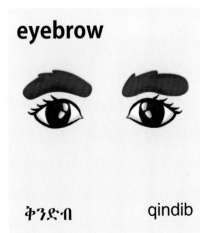
ቅንድብ   qindib

a b c d e f g h i j k l m n o p q r s t u v w x y z

Ff

fabric

ጨርቅ   cherk

face

ፊት   fit

factory

ፋብሪካ   fabrika

fairy

ቸር መንፈስ
cher menfes

family

ቤተሰብ   beteseb

fan

ማራገቢያ   maragebiya

farm

እርሻ   'èrsha

farmer

ገበሬ   gebere

fat

ወፍራም   wefram

father

አባት   abat

feather

ላባ   laba

female

ሴት   set

fence

አጥር   atir

ferry

ጀልባ   jelba

field

ሜዳ   meda

fig

በለስ   beles

file

ፋይል   fayl

film

ፊልም   film

finger

ጣት   tat

fire

እሳት   isat

fire engine

የእሳት አደጋ መኪና
yeisat adega mekina

firefighter

የእሳት አደጋ አጥፊ
yeisat adega atifi

fireworks

ርችት   richit

fish

አሳ asa

fist

ቡጢ buïi

five

አምስት amist

flag

ባንዲራ bandira

flame

ነበልባል nebelbal

flamingo

ፍላሚንጎ flamingo

flask

ፋሽኮ fashiko

flock

መንጋ menga

flood

ጎርፍ gorf

floor

ወለል welel

florist

አበባ ሻጭ
abeba shach

flour

ዱቄት duqeet

flower

አበባ   abeba

flute

ዋሽንት   washint

fly

ዝንብ   zinb

foam

አረፋ   arefa

fog

ጉም   gum

foil

ፎይል   foyl

food

ምግብ   migb

foot

እግር   egir

football
US English **soccer**

የእግር ኩአስ
ye egir kuas

forearm

ክንድ   kend

forehead

ግንባር   ginbar

forest

ደን   den

a b c d e f g h i J k l m n o p q r s t u v w x y z

fork

ሹካ shuka

fortress

ምሽግ mishig

fountain

ምንጭ mnč

four

4

አራት arat

fox

ቀበሮ qebero

frame

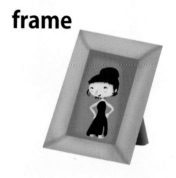

ክፈፍ kfef

freezer

ማቀዝቀዣአ
makezkeza

fridge
US English **refrigerator**

ፍሪጅ frij

friend

ጓደኛ guadegna

frog

እንቁራሪት enkurarit

fruit

ፍራፍሬ firafire

fumes

ጢስ tis

funnel

ማጥለያ   matileya

furnace

እቶን   eton

furniture

የቤት እቃ
yebet eka

Gg

gadget

መግብር   megbr

gallery

የስእል አዳራሽ
ye seel adarash

game

ጨዋታ   chewata

gap

ባዶ ቦታ   bado bota

garage

ጋራዥ   garaz

garbage

ቆሻሻ   koshasha

garden

የአትክልት ቦታ
ye atikilt bota

garland

ጉንጉን   gungun

garlic

ነጭ ሽንኩርት
nech shinkurt

gas

ጋዝ   gaz

gate

በር   ber

gem

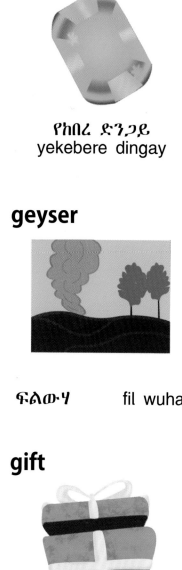

የከበረ ድንጋይ
yekebere dingay

generator

ጄኔሬተር   jenereter

germ

ጀርም   jerm

geyser

ፍልውሃ   fil wuha

ghost

ጣረሞት   taremot

giant

ግዙፍ   guzuf

gift

ስጦታ   sitota

ginger

ዝንጅብል   zinjibl

giraffe

ቀጭኔ   kechine

a b c d e f **g** h i J k l m n o p q r s t u v w x y z

36

girl

ልጃገረድ   lijagered

glacier

የበረዶ ወንዝ
yeberedo wenz

glass

መስታወት   mestawet

glider

ያለ ሞተር በአየር ተንሳፋፊ
yale moter be'eyer
tensafufi

globe

ሉል   lul

glove

ጓንት   guant

glue

ሙጫ   mucha

goal

ግብ   gib

goat

ፍየል   fiyel

gold

ወርቅ   werk

golf

ጎልፍ   golfi

goose

ዝይ   ziy

a b c d e f g h i j k l m n o p q r s t u v w x y z

37

gorilla

ገመሬ   gemeree

grain

እህል   'èhl

grandfather

ወንድ አያት
wend ayat

grandmother

ሴት አያት   set ayat

grape

ወይን   weyn

grapefruit

እንድ ዓይነት ፍሬ
'end 'äynet free

grass

ሳር   sar

grasshopper

ፌንጣ   feenta

gravel

ጠጠር   teter

green

አረንጉዬ   arenguade

grey

ግራጫ   giracha

grill

የብረት ምድጃ
yebiret midija

grocery

የሽቀጣሽቀጥ
yesheqetasheqet

ground

መሬት meret

guard

ጠባቂ tebaki

guava

ባባ vava

guide

መመሪያ memeriya

guitar

ጊታር gitar

gulf

ባህረሰላጤ
bahreselatee

gun

ጠበንጃ tebenja

gypsy

ጂፕሲ jipisi

Hh

hair

ፀጉር tsegur

hairbrush

ፀጉር ብሩሽ
tsegur burush

hairdresser

የፀጉር አስተካካይ
ye tsegur astekakay

half

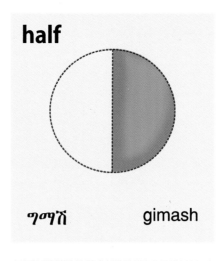

ግማሽ   gimash

hall

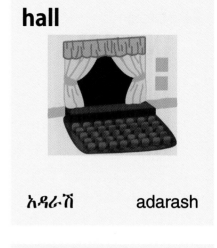

አዳራሽ   adarash

ham

የታጠነ የአሳማ ወርች
yetatene yeasama werch

hammer

መዶሻ   medosha

hammock

ጀርሞሽ   jermosh

hand

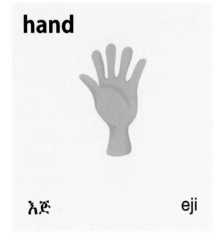

እጅ   eji

handbag

ቦርሳ   borsa

handicraft

የእጅ ሥራ ye eji sira

handkerchief

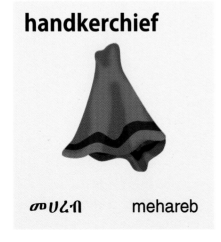

መሀረብ   mehareb

handle

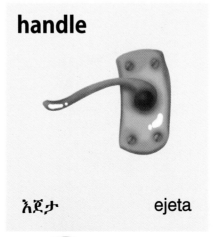

እጀታ   ejeta

hanger

መስቀያ   mesqeya

harbour
US English **harbor**

ወደብ   wedeb

hare

ጥንቸል   tinchel

harvest

አዝመራ   azimera

hat

ባርኔጣ   barneta

hawk

ጭልፊት   chilfit

hay

ድርቆሽ   dirkosh

head

ራስ   ras

headphone

የጆሮ ማዳመጫ
yejoro madamecha

heap

ክምር   kimir

heart

ልብ   lib

heater

ማሞቂያ   mamokiya

hedge

ቁጥቋጦ   kutikwato

a b c d e f g **h** i j k l m n o p q r s t u v w x y z

heel

ተረከዝ terekez

helicopter

ሂሊኮፕተር hilikopter

helmet

የራስ ቁር yeras qur

hen

ዶሮ doro

herb

እፅ' èx

herd

መንጋ menga

hermit

ባህታዊ bahtawi

hill

ኮረብታ korebta

hippopotamus

ጉማሬ gumare

hive

ቀፎ qefo

hole

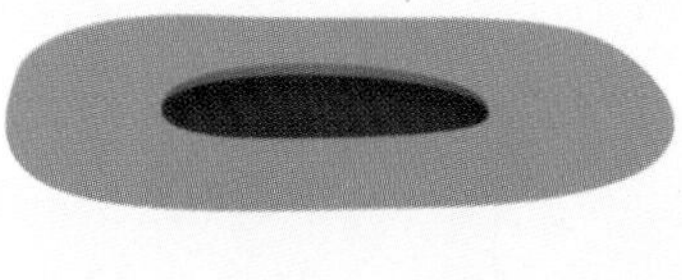

ቀዳዳ qedada

honey

ማር mar

hood
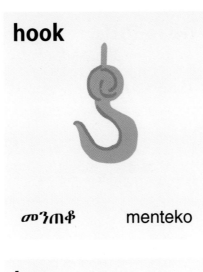
ቆብ   qob

hook
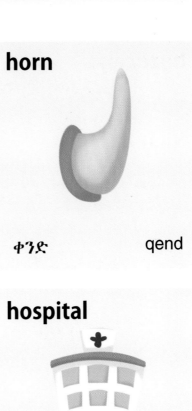
መንጠቆ   menteko

horn

ቀንድ   qend

horse

ፈረስ   feres

hose
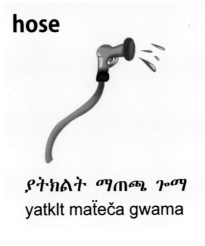
ያትክልት ማጠጫ ጐማ
yatklt maïeča gwama

hospital

ሐኪም ቤት
hakimi beet

hotdog

ሆት ደግ   hoti dog

hotel

ሆቴል   hotel

hour

ሰአት   seaat

house

ቤት   bet

human

ሰው   sew

hunter

አዳኝ   adagn

a
b
c
d
e
f
g
h
i
j
k
l
m
n
o
p
q
r
s
t
u
v
w
x
y
z

hurricane

አውሎ ነፋስ
awilo nifas

husband

ባል   bal

hut

ጎጆ   gojo

Ii

ice

በረዶ   beredo

iceberg

ትልቅ የበረዶ ሰባሪ
tlq yeberedo sebari

ice cream

አይስክሬም
ayis krem

idol

ጣዖት   taot

igloo

ከበረዶ የሚሰራ ቤት
keberedo yemisera bet

inch

ኢንች   einchi

injection

መርፌ   merfe

injury
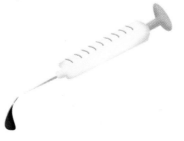
ጉዳት   gudat

44

ink

ቀለም   kelem

inn

ትንሽ ሆቴል
tinsh hotel

insect

ነፍሳት   nefisat

inspector

መርማሪ   mermari

instrument

መሳሪያ   mesariya

internet

ኢንተርኔት
enternet

intestine

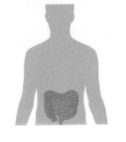

አንጀት   anjet

inventor

ፈጣሪ   fetari

invitation

ጥሪ   ẗri

iron

ብረት   biret

island

ደሴት   deset

ivory

የዝሆን ጥርስ
yezihon tirs

Jj

jackal

ቀበሮ   kebero

jacket

ጃኬት   jaket

jackfruit

ጃክፍሩት   jaqifrut

jam

ማርማላት   marmalat

jar

እንስራ   inisira

javelin

ጦር   tor

jaw

መንጋጋ   mengaga

jeans

ጂንስ   jins

jelly

የፍሬ ገንፎ
yefree genfo

jetty

ወደብ   wedeb

jewellery
US English **jewelry**

ጌጣጌጥ   getaget

jigsaw

አግኝቻለሁ
'egǹchalehu

jockey

ፈረሰኛ   fereseǹa

joker

ቀልደኛ   qeldegna

journey

ጉዞ   guzo

jug

ደምበጃን   dembejan

juggler

በእጁ እንቅስቃሴ የሚያዝናና ሰው
be eju enkiskase
yemiyaznana sew

juice

ጭማቂ   čmaqi

jungle

ጫካ   chaka

jute

የጅራ   yejira

kangaroo

ካንጋሮ   kangaro

kennel

የውሻ ቤት
ye wusha bet

Kk

a b c d e f g h i **J** **k** l m n o p q r s t u v w x y z

abcdefghiJklmnopqrstuvwxyz

kerb
US English **curb**

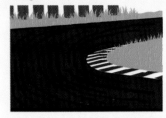

ኩርባ   kurba

kerosene

ነጭ ጋዝ
nechi gaz

ketchup

የቲማቲም ድልህ
ye timatim dilh

kettle

ጀበና   jebena

key

ቁልፍ   qulf

keyboard

ኪቦርድ   kibord

key ring

ቁልፍ መያዣ
qulf meyaźa

kidney

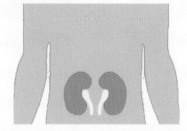

ኩላሊት   kulalit

kilogram

ኪሎግራም   kilogram

king

ንጉስ   nigus

kiosk

ትንሽ ሱቅ   tinsh suk

kiss

መሳም   mesam

kitchen
ማድቤት madbet

kite
ወላንዶ welando

kitten
ግልገል gilgel

kiwi
ኪዊ kiwi

knee
ጉልበት gulbet

knife
ቢላ bila

knight
ባላባት balabat

knitwear
ጥልፍ ልብስ tilf libs

knob
እጀታ ejeta

knock
አንኳኳ ankuakua

knot
ቋጠሮ quaterro

knuckle
የጣቶች መጋጠሚያ
ye tatoch megatemiya

a
b
c
d
e
f
g
h
i
j
J
k
l
m
n
o
p
q
r
s
t
u
v
w
x
y
z

Ll

label

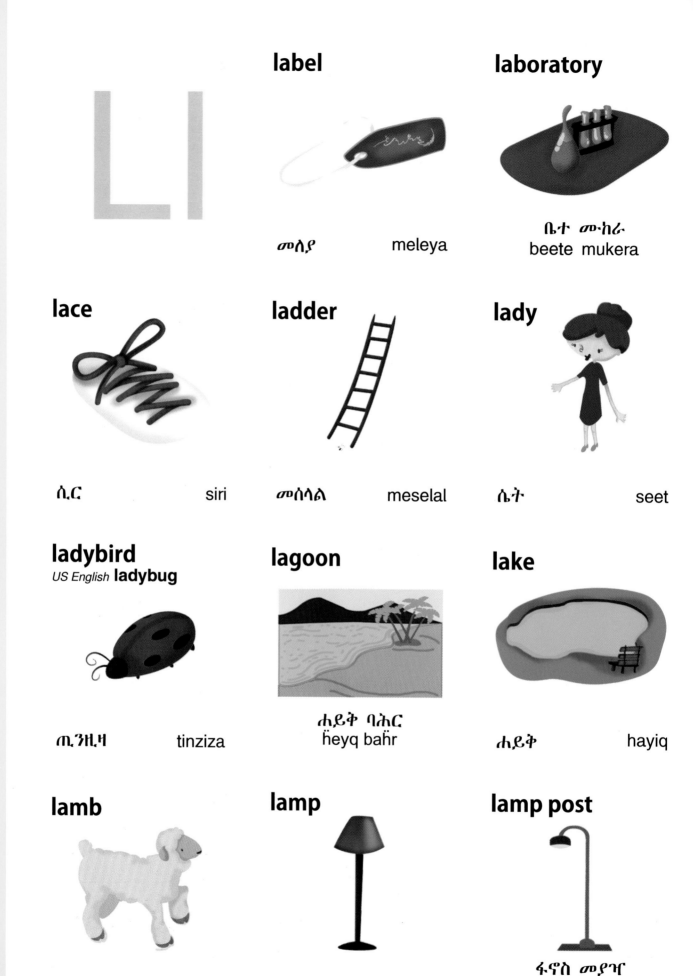

መለያ   meleya

laboratory

ቤት ሙከራ
beete mukera

lace

ሲር   siri

ladder

መሰላል   meselal

lady

ሴት   seet

ladybird
US English **ladybug**

ጢንዚዛ   tinziza

lagoon

ሐይቅ ባሕር
ḧeyq baḧr

lake

ሐይቅ   hayiq

lamb

ጠቦት   tebot

lamp

መብራት   mebirat

lamp post

ፋኖስ መያዣ
fanos meyaza

land

መሬት   meret

lane

መንገድ   menged

lantern

ፋኖስ   fanos

laser

ሌዘር   lezer

lasso

ያልባሉ   yalbalu

latch

መወርወርያ
mewerwerya

laundry

የልብስ ማጠቢያ ቦታ
yelbs maẗebiya bota

lawn

ግቢውን   gbiwn

lawyer

ጠበቃ   tebeka

layer
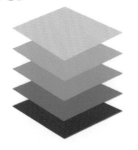
ንብርብር   nibiribir

leaf

ቅጠል   qitel

leather

ቆዳ   qoda

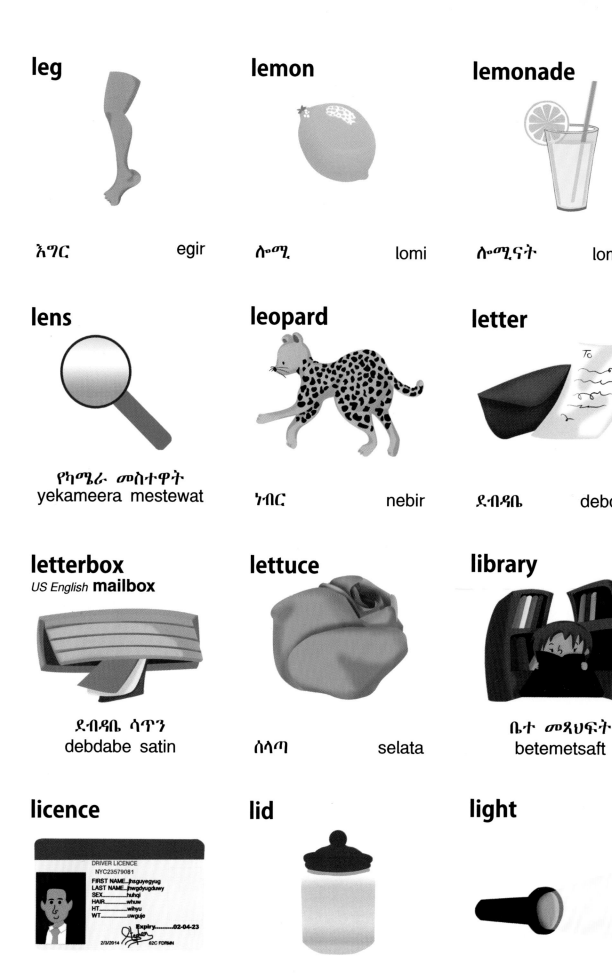

leg

እግር egir

lemon

ሎሚ lomi

lemonade

ሎሚናት lominat

lens

የካሜራ መስተዋት
yekameera mestewat

leopard

ነብር nebir

letter

ደብዳቤ debdabe

letterbox
US English **mailbox**

ደብዳቤ ሳጥን
debdabe satin

lettuce

ሰላጣ selata

library

ቤተ መጻህፍት
betemetsaft

licence

ፍቃድ fkad

lid

ክዳን kidan

light

ብርሀን brhan

lighthouse

የፋና ቤት
yefuna beet

limb

እጅና እግር   ejina egir

line

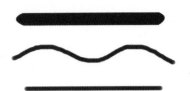

መስመር   mesmer

lion

አንበሳ   anbesaa

lip

ከንፈር   kenfer

lipstick

ሊፕስቲክ   lipstik

liquid

ፈሳሽ   fesash

list

ዝርዝር   zirzir

litre
US English **liter**

ሊትር   litr

living room

ሳሎን   salon

lizard

እንሽላሊት   enshilalit

load

ጫና   čana

a b c d e f g h i J k l m n o p q r s t u v w x y z

loaf

እንጀራ 'ènĵera

lobster

ሎብስተር lobisteri

lock

መቆለፊያ meqolefiya

loft

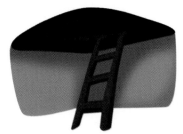

ክፍል kfl

log

ሳንቃ sanqa

loop

የቀለበት ቅርጽ
yeqelebet qrts

lorry
US English **truck**

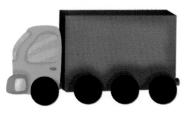

የጭነት መኪና
yechinet mekina

lotus

የባህር ዳር አበባ
yebahr dar abeba

louse

ቅማል qimal

luggage

ሻንጣ shanta

lunch

ምሳ misa

lung

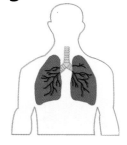

ሳንባ sanba

Mm

machine
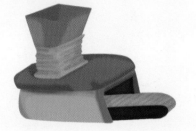
ማሽን   mashin

magazine

መጽሄት   metsihet

magician

ጠንቋይ   tenqway

magnet

መግነጢስ   megnetis

magpie

ነጭና ጥቁር ወፍ
nechna tqur wef

mail
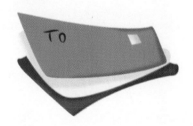
ፖስታ   posta

mammal

በወተት ታዳጊ እንስሳ
bewetet tadagi 'ènssa

man

ሰው   sew

mandolin

ማንዶሊን   mandolin

mango

ማንጎ   mango

map

ካርታ   karta

a b c d e f g h i j J k l m n o p q r s t u v w x y z

maple

የሜፕል   yemeepl

marble

እብነ በረድ
ebne bered

market

ገበያ   gebeya

mask

ጭንብል   chinbil

mast

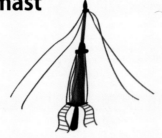

የመርከብ ተራዳ
yemerkeb terada

mat

ሰሌን   seleen

matchbox

ክብሪት   kibrit

mattress

ፍራሽ   firash

meal

ምግብ   megib

meat

ስጋ   siga

mechanic

ሜካኒሲያን
meekanisiyan

medicine

መድሃኒት   medanit

melon

ከርቡሽ   kerbush

merchant

ነጋዴ   negade

mermaid

አንድ መልአክ ዓሣ
ānidi meli'āki 'aša

metal

ብረት   biret

metre
US English **meter**

ሜትር   metir

microphone

ማይክሮፎን
maykrofon

microwave

ማይክሮዌቭ
maykrowev

mile

ማይል   mayil

milk

ወተት   wetet

miner

ማእድን አውጪ
mayidn awchi

mineral

ማእድን   mayidin

mint

ከአዝሙድና
ke'ezmudna

mud

ጭቃ   chika

muffin

ኬክ   kek

mug

ምሳና   msana

mule

በቅሎ   beqlo

muscle

ጡንቻ   tuncha

museum

ቤተ መዘክር
beete mezekr

mushroom

እንጉዳይ   enguday

music

ሙዚቃ   muzika

musician

ሙዚቀኛ   muzikegna

Nn

nail

ምስማር   mismar

napkin

የገበታ ፎጣ
yegebeta foïa

nappy
US English **diaper**

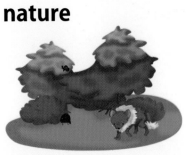

የበሰለ   yebesele

nature

ተፈጥሮ   tefetro

neck

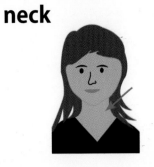

አንገት   anget

necklace

የአንገት ጌጥ
ye anget get

necktie

ከረባት   kerevat

needle

መርፌ   merfe

neighbour
US English **neighbor**

ጎረቤት   gorebet

nest

የወፍ ጎጆ
ye wef gojo

net

መረብ   mereb

newspaper

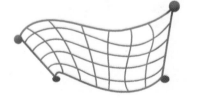

ጋዜጣ   gazeta

night

ሌሊት   lelit

nine

ዘጠኝ   zetegn

a b c d e f g h i j k l m **n** o p q r s t u v w x y z

a b c d e f g h i j k l m **n** o p q r s t u v w x y z

noodles

ፓስታዎች
pastawoch

noon

ቀትር   qetir

north
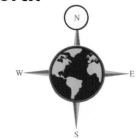
ሰሜን   semen

nose
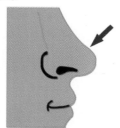
አፍንጫ   afincha

note

ማስታወሻ
mastawesha

notebook

ማስታወሻ ደብተር
mastawesha debter

notice
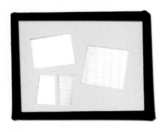
ማስታወቂያ
mastaweqiya

number
0 1 2 3
ቁጥር   qutir

nun

መነኩሲት   menekusit

nurse

አስታመመ
'estameme

nursery

መዋዕለ ሕፃናት
mewale hitsanat

nut

ለውዝ   lewiz

Oo

oar

መቅዘፊያ
meqzefiya

observatory
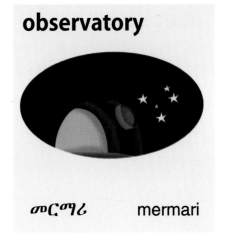
መርማሪ mermari

ocean
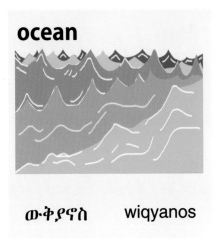
ውቅያኖስ wiqyanos

octopus
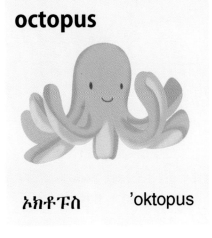
ኦክቶፑስ 'oktopus

office

ቢሮ biro

oil

ዘይት zeyit

olive

የወይራ ፍሬ
yeweyra fire

omelette

የእንቁላል ጥብስ
ye enkulal tibs

one

አንድ andi

onion

ሽንኩርት shinkurt

orange
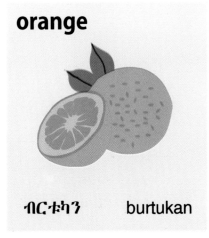
ብርቱካን burtukan

a b c d e f g h i J k l m n o p q r s t u v w x y z

a b c d e f g h i j J k l m n o p q r s t u v w x y z

orbit

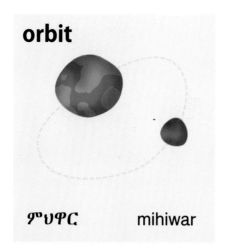

ምህዋር   mihiwar

orchard

የፍራፍሬ እርሻ
yefirafre ersha

orchestra

የሙዚቃ ጓድ
yemuziqa gwad

ostrich

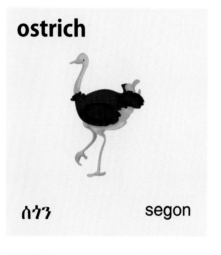

ሰጎን   segon

otter

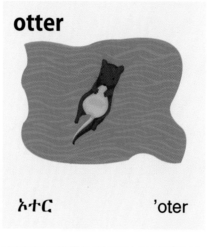

ኦተር   'oter

oval

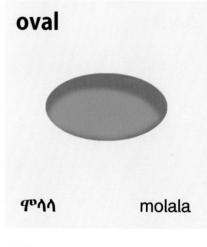

ሞላላ   molala

oven

ምድጃ   midija

owl

ጉጉት   gugut

ox

በሬ   bere

Pp

packet

ፓኬት   pakeet

page

ገጽ   getse

pain

ጣረሞት   ťaremot

paint
ቀለም   qelem

painting
ስዕል   seel

pair
ጥንድ   tind

palace
ቤተመንግስት
betemengst

palm
መዳፍ   medaf

pan
መጥበሻ   metbesha

pancake
ፓንኬክ   pankek

panda
ፓንዳ   panda

papaya
ፓፓያ   papaye

paper
ወረቀት   wereket

parachute
ፓራቹት   poravut

a b c d e f g h i j k l m n o p q r s t u v w x y z

parcel

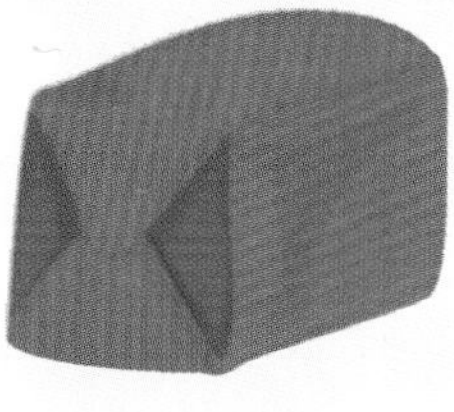

ጥቅልል ጥቅል
ẗqll ẗql

park

መናፈሻ   menafesha

parrot

በቅበቃ   beqbeqa

passenger

መንገደኛ
mengedegna

pasta

ፓስታ   pasta

pastry

ኬክ   kek

pavement

መንገድ   menged

paw

እግር   'ègr

pea

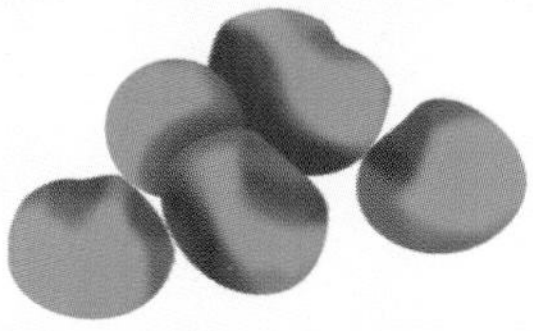

አተር   ater

peach

ኮክ   kok

peacock

ጣዎስ   ẗawos

peak

ጫፍ   chaf

66

peanut
ለውዝ   lewiz

pear
ሽክኒት   sheknit

pearl
ሉል   lul

pedal
እርካብ   'èrkab

pelican
ይብራ   ybra

pen
ብዕር   b'ër

pencil
እርሳስ   ersas

penguin
ፔንግዊን   pēnigiwīni

pepper
በርበሬ   berberee

perfume
ሽቶ   shito

pet
የቤት እንስሳ   yebet ensissa

pharmacy
መድሃኒት ቤት   medhanit bet

a b c d e f g h i j k l m n o **p** q r s t u v w x y z

photograph
ፎቶግራፍ
fotograf

piano
ፒያኖ
piyano

picture
ሥዕል
's'ël

pie
ኬክ
keek

pig
አሳማ
asama

pigeon
እርግብ
ergib

pillar
አምድ
'emd

pillow
ትራስ
tiras

pilot
አብራሪ
abrari

pineapple
አናናስ
ananas

pink
ሐምራዊ
ĥemrawi

pipe
ቧምቧ
bwamibwa

pizza
ፒዛ piza

planet
ፕላኔት pilanet

plant
ተክል tekil

plate
ሳህን sahn

platform
መድረክ medrek

platypus
ፕላትቲፕስ
platipls

player
ተጫዋች techawach

plum
እንኩይ enkway

plumber
ቧንቧ ጠጋኝ
bwanibwa teganyi

plywood
ኮምፔንሳቶ
kompensato

pocket
ኪስ kis

poet
ገጣሚ getami

polar bear

የበርዶ ድብ
yeberedo dib

police

ፖሊስ   polis

pollution

ብክለት   biklet

pomegranate

ሮማን   roman

pond

ኩሬ   kure

porcupine

ጃርት   jarit

port

ወደብ   wedeb

porter

በረኛ   bereǹa

postcard

ፖስታ   posta

postman

የፖስታ አዳይ
yeposta 'eday

post office

ፖስታ ቤት   posta bet

pot

ማሰሮ   masero

70

potato

ድንች   dinich

powder

ዱቄት   duket

prawn

ተበክሎባቻዋል
tebeklobachewal

priest

ቄስ   qes

prince

ልኡል   liuel

prison

ዘብጥያ   zebtya

pudding

ፑዲንግ   puding

pump

መንፊያ   menfiya

pumpkin

ዱባ   duba

puppet

አሻንጉሊት   ashangulit

puppy

ቡችላ   buchla

purse

ከረጢት   keretit

Qq

quail

ድርጭቶች
drčtoch

quarry

ካብ   kab

queen

ንግስት   nigist

queue

ረድፍ   redf

quiver

ሰገባ   segeba

Rr

rabbit

ጥንቸል   tinchel

rack

መደርደሪያ
madardariya

racket

ራኬት   raketi

radio

ሬድዮ   rediyo

radish

ፍጁል   fjul

raft

ታንኳ   tankua

rain

ዝናብ   zinab

rainbow

ቀስተ ደመና
qeste demena

raisin

ዘቢብ   zebib

ramp

መንሽራተቻ
mensheratecha

raspberry

እንጆሪ   enjori

rat

አይጥ   ayit

razor

ምላጭ   milach

receipt

ደረሰኝ   deresegn

rectangle

አራት ማዕዘን
arat maezen

red

ቀይ   qey

restaurant

ምግብ ቤት
migb bet

a b c d e f g h i j k l m n o p q **r** s t u v w x y z

73

rhinoceros

አውራሪስ
awraris

rib

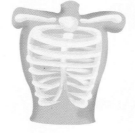

የጎድን አጥንት
yegodin atint

ribbon

ጥብጣብ   tibitab

rice

ሩዝ   ruz

ring

ቀለበት   qelebet

river

ወንዝ   wenz

road

መንገድ   menged

robber

ዘራፊ   zerafi

robe

መጎናጸፊያ
megwanaxefiya

robot

ሮቦት   robot

rock

አለት   alet

rocket

ሮኬት   roket

roller coaster

ተጠቅላይ ተወርዋሪ
teteklay tewerwari

room

ክፍል   kifl

root

ስር   sir

rope

ገመድ   gemed

rose

ጽጌሬዳ   tsigereda

round

ክብ   kib

rug

ምንጣፍ   mintaf

rugby

ራግቢ   ragbi

ruler

ማስመሪያ
masimeriya

Ss

sack

ጆንያ   jonya

sail

የመርከብ ሸራ
yemerkeb shera

abcdefghijklmnopq**s**tuvwxyz

sailor

መርከበኛ
merkebegna

salad

ሰላጣ   selata

salt

ጨው   chew

sand

አሸዋ   ashewa

sandwich

ሳንድዊች   sandwich

satellite

ሳተላይት   satelayt

saucer

የስኒ ማስቀመጫ
yesini maskemecha

sausage

ቋሊማ   qualima

saw

መጋዝ   megaz

scarf

ሻሽ   shash

school

ትምህርት ቤት
timhrt bet

scissors

መቀስ   meqes

76

scooter
ብስክሌቱ   bskleetu

scorpion
ጊንጥ   gint

screw
ብሎን   blon

sea
ባሕር   bahir

seal
ባህር እንስሳ
bahiri inisesa

seat
መቀመጫ   meqemeča

see-saw
ሚዛን መጫወቻ
mizan mechawecha

seven
ሰባት   sebat

shadow
ጥላ   tila

shampoo
ሻምፑ   shampu

shark
ሻርክ   shariki

sheep
በግ   beg

a b c d e f g h i j J k l m n o p q r s t u v w x y z

shelf

መደርደሪያ
mederderya

shell

ቀፎ   qefo

shelter

መጠለያ   meteleya

ship

መርከብ   merkeb

shirt

ሸሚዝ   shemiz

shoe

ጫማ   chama

shorts

ቁምጣ   qumta

shoulder

ትከሻ   tkesha

shower

የቁም መታጠቢያ ቤት
yequm metaẗebiya beet

shutter

መስኮት መዝጊያ
meskot mezgiya

shuttlecock

የባድሚንተን መጫወቻ ኳስ
yebadminten
mechawecha kwas

signal

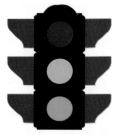

ምልክት   milkit

silver
ብር   bir

sink
ብርት   birit

sister
እህት   ehit

six
ስድስት   sidist

skate
ተንሽራተተ
tensheratete

skeleton
አጽም   atsim

ski
የእንጪት መንሽራተቻ
ye'ènčit mensheratecha

skin
ቆዳ   qoda

skirt
ሽሚዝ   shemiz

skull
የራስ ቅል   years kil

sky
ሰማይ   semay

skyscraper
ሰማይ ጠቀስ ፎቅ
semay teqes foq

slide

መንሸራተት
mensheratet

slipper

የቤት ጫማ
yebeet čama

smoke

ጭስ   chis

snail

ቀንድ አውጣ
kend awta

snake

እባብ   ebab

snow

በረዶ   beredo

soap

ሳሙና   samuna

sock

ካልሲ   kalsi

sofa

ሶፋ   sofa

soil

አፈር   afer

soldier

ወታደር   wetader

soup

ሾርባ   shorba

space
ሀዋ   hiwa

spaghetti
ስፓጌቲ   spageti

sphere
ሉል   lul

spider
ሸረሪት   shererit

spinach
ቆስጣ   kosta

sponge
ሰፍነግ   sefneg

spoon
ማንኪያ   mankiya

spray
ርብርብ   ribrib

spring
ፀደይ   tsedey

square
አራት መአዘን
'erat me'ezen

squirrel
ሽኮኮ   shekako

stadium
ስታዲየም   stadiyem

a b c d e f g h i J k l m n o p q r **s** t u v w x y z

a b c d e f g h i j k l m n o p q r s t u v w x y z

stairs
ደረጃ   dereja

stamp
ቴምብር   tembir

star
ኮከብ   kokeb

station
ኬላ   keela

statue
ሐውልት   hawiliti

stethoscope
ማዳመጫ   madamecha

stomach
ሆድ   hod

stone
ድንጋይ   dingay

storm
አውሎ   'ewlo

straw
ገለባ   geleba

strawberry
እንጆሪ   enjori

street
መንገድ   menged

student

ተማሪ temari

submarine

ሰርጎ ገብ ጀልባ
sergo geb jelba

subway

ባቡር ጋለርያ
babur galerya

sugar

ስኳር skuar

sugarcane

ሸንኮራ አገዳ
shenkora ageda

summer

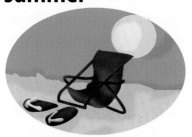

በጋ bega

sun

ፀሐይ tsehay

supermarket

ሱፐርማርኬት
supamarqet

swan

ዳክዬ dakyee

sweet

ጣፋጭ tafach

swimming pool

መዋኛ ገንዳ
mewagna genda

swimsuit

የዋና ልብስ
yewana libs

swing

ሽዋሽዌ   ziwaziwe

switch

ማብሪያ ማጥፊያ
mabriya matfat

syrup

ሽሮፕ   shurop

Tt

table

ጠረጴዛ   terepeza

tall

ረጅም   rejim

tank

ታንክ   tank

taxi

ታክሲ   taksi

tea

ሻይ   shay

teacher

መምህር   memhir

teeth

ጥርስ   tirs

telephone

ስልክ   silk

television

ቴሌቪዥን   televshn

ten

አስር   asir

tennis

ቴኒስ   tenis

tent

ድንኳን   dinkuan

thief

ሌባ   leba

thread

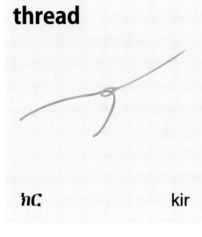

ክር   kir

three

ሶስት   sosit

throat

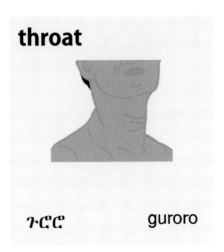

ጉሮሮ   guroro

thumb

አውራ ጣት
awra tat

ticket

ቲኬት   tiket

tiger

ነብር   nebir

toe

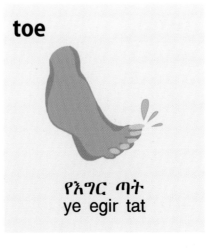

የእግር ጣት
ye egir tat

a b c d e f g h i j J k l m n o p q r s **t** u v w x y z

tofu

ቶፉ   tofu

tomato

ቲማቲም   timatim

tongue

ምላስ   milas

tool

መሣሪያ   mesariya

toothbrush

ፋቅ   faq

toothpaste

የጥርስ ሳሙና
yetiris samuna

tortoise

ኤሊ   eli

towel

ፎጣ   fota

tower

ግንብ   ginib

toy

መጫወቻ
mečawecha

tractor

ማረሻ መኪና
maresha mekina

train

ባቡር   babur

tree

ዛፍ   zaf

triangle

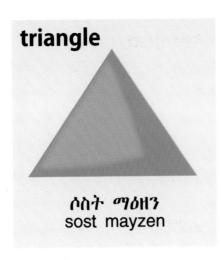

ሶስት ማዕዘን
sost mayzen

tub

የእንጪት በርሚል
ye'ènčit bermil

tunnel

የመሬት ውስጥ መንገድ
yemereet wsт menged

turnip

ፍጁል   fjul

tyre

US English **tire**

ጎማ   goma

Uu

umbrella

ዝንጥላ   zantila

uncle

አጎት   agot

uniform

የደንብ ልብስ
yedenib libis

university

ዩኒቨርሲቲ
yuniversity

utensil

የወጥ ቤት መሳሪያ
yewet beet mesariya

a b c d e f g h i j k l m n o p q r s t u v w x y z

Vv

vacuum cleaner

የኤሌክትሪክ ፍራፍ
ye'ēlēkitirīki firafi

valley

ሸለቆ   sheleko

van

የጭነት መኪና
yechnet mekina

vase

የአበባ ማስቀመጫ
yeabeba maskemecha

vault

ካዝና   kazna

vegetable

አትክልት   atikilt

veil

መሸፈኛ   meshefeǹa

vet

የእንስሳት ሀኪም
ye'ensisat hakim

village

መንደር   mender

violet

ሀምራዊ   hamrawi

violin

ቫዮሊን   vayolin

volcano

እሳተ ገሞራ
esate gemora

volleyball

መረብ ኳስ
mereb kwas

vulture

ጥንብ አንሳ   tinb ansa

Ww

waist

ወገብ   wegeb

waitress

አስተናጋጅ   astenagaj

wall
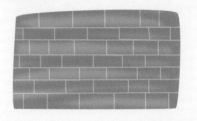
ግድግዳ   gidgida

wallet

የኪስ ቦርሳ
yekis borsa

walnut

ለውዝ   lewiz

wand

የአስማተኞች በትር
yeasmatenyoch betr

wardrobe

የልብስ መስቀያ
yelbs mesqeya

warehouse
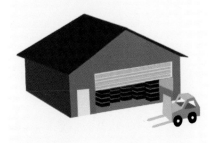
መጋዘን   megazen

a
b
c
d
e
f
g
h
i
j
k
l
m
n
o
p
q
r
s
t
u
v
w
x
y
z

wasp

ተርብ   terb

watch

የግድግዳ ሰዓት
yegidigida seati

water

ውሃ   wuha

watermelon

ሀብሀብ   habhab

web

ድር   dir

whale

አሳነባሪ   asanebari

wheat

ስንዴ   sinde

wheel

መንኮራኩር
menkorakur

whistle

ፉጨት   fuchet

white

ነጭ   nech

wife

ሚስት   mist

window

መስኮት   meskot

wing

ክንፍ   kinf

winter

ክረምት   kiremt

wizard

አዋቂ   'ewaqi

wolf

ተኩላ   tekula

woman

ሴት   set

woodpecker

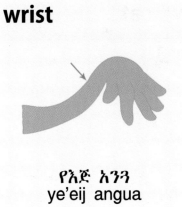

ግንደቆርቁር
gindeqorkur

wool

ሱፍ   suf

workshop

መሥሪያ   me'sriya

wrist

የእጅ አንጓ
ye'eij angua

x-ray

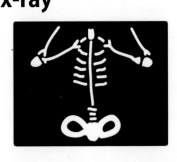

ኤክስሬይ   exrey

xylophone

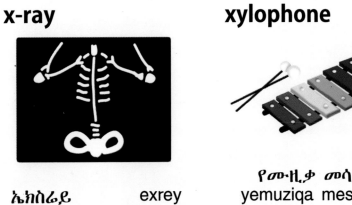

የሙዚቃ መሳሪያ
yemuziqa mesariya

Xx

Yy

yacht

አነስተኛ መርከብ
enesteṅa merkeb

yak

በሬ መሳይ እንስሳ
bere mesay enssa

yard
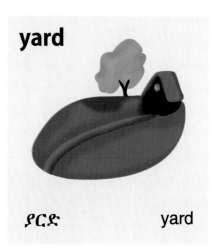
ያርድ
yard

yellow

ቢጫ
bicha

yoghurt

ዮጉርት
yogurt

Zz

zebra

የሜዳ አህያ
yemeda ahiya

zero

ዜሮ
zero

zip

ዚፕ
zipi

zodiac

የዞዲያክ
yezodiyak

zoo

መንበሪ አራዊት
meniberī ārawīti